SAP HANA Starter

Everything you need to know to be able to build your first
SAP HANA standalone application!

Mark Walker

BIRMINGHAM - MUMBAI

SAP HANA Starter

First published: November 2012

Production Reference: 1141112

Published by Packt Publishing Ltd.
Livery Place
35 Livery Street
Birmingham B3 2PB, UK.

ISBN 978-1-84968-868-0

www.packtpub.com

Credits

Author

Mark Walker

Reviewers

Alvaro Tejada Galindo

William Grosjean

Stéphane PARISIS

Acquisition Editor

Erol Staveley

Commissioning Editor

Ameya Sawant

Technical Editor

Dominic Pereira

Project Coordinator

Amigya Khurana

Proofreader

Jonathan Todd

Production Coordinator

Prachali Bhiwandkar

Cover Work

Prachali Bhiwandkar

Cover Image

Conidon Miranda

About the author

Mark Walker has been an SAP technical consultant for over 16 years, starting with ERP, in the ABAP programming area, where he specialized in bespoke programming and optimization. Next up came the BW Business Intelligence platform, again specializing in hard-to-implement solutions, especially in the SEM-BPS and BI-IP (integrated planning—or how to write user data into a cube) modules. He's been working with SAP HANA since 2011 just after it was released, and is a certified Application Associate on HANA since early 2012.

About the reviewer

Alvaro Tejada Galindo, also known as "Blag", has experience as an ABAP Senior Consultant for 11 years. Currently he works as a Development Expert for the Developer Experience team at SAP Labs Montreal focusing on Technology Evangelism and Developer Engagement.

> I would like to thanks my wife Milly and my daughter Kiara for all their support and patience when I was doing the technical review of this book.

William Grosjean is senior architect and program manager on BI and Analytics. With 15 years spent on SAP platforms, he started with ERP, in the ABAP programming area, then rapidly moved to architecture and system administration. Upskilled in BI & Analytics in 2003, he has been working as principal business consultant on BI and Analytics for SAP France during the last four years. With a strong expertise on BW and BusinessObjects platform, he had the chance to run the first HANA proof-of-concept in France for a large account in Utilities in early 2011 during the ramp-up phase of the product. William is now heading the BI & EPM consulting company BMB Services, addressing all industries on In-Memory technologies. He is a certified Application Associate on HANA since early 2012.

Stéphane PARISIS has 13 years of experience in controlling, reporting, and budget planning, in the industry, media, consumer goods, utilities, and public sectors. He is a SAP expert in controlling areas with cross understanding of financial impacts on the other SAP related modules (SD/MM/PP), SAP BI / BusinessObjects, and the EPM implementation manager. He is also SAP certified.

He works for BMB services, which is a BI & EPM consulting company, specializing in functional business requirements and program management. After facing growing demand on mobility and agility from their customers, his company is continuously renewing their BI market knowledge and expertise in order to better promote the best breed of BI solutions.

www.PacktPub.com

Support files, eBooks, discount offers, and more

You might want to visit www.PacktPub.com for support files and downloads related to your book.

Did you know that Packt Publishing offers eBook versions of every book published, with PDF and ePub files available? You can upgrade to the eBook version at www.PacktPub.com and as a print book customer, you are entitled to a discount on the eBook copy. Get in touch with us at service@packtpub.com for more details.

At www.PacktPub.com, you can also read a collection of free technical articles, sign up for a range of free newsletters, and receive exclusive discounts and offers on Packt Publishing books and eBooks.

Instant Updates on New Packt Books

Get notified! Find out when new books are published by following @PacktEnterprise on Twitter, or the *Packt Enterprise* Facebook page.

www.PacktLib.PacktPub.com

Do you need instant solutions to your IT questions? PacktLib is Packt's online digital book library. Here, you can access, read and search across Packt's entire library of books.

Why Subscribe?

- ✦ Fully searchable across every book published by Packt
- ✦ Copy and paste, print, and bookmark content
- ✦ On demand and accessible via web browser

Free Access for Packt Publishing account holders

If you have an account with Packt at www.PacktPub.com, you can use this to access PacktLib today and view nine entirely free books. Simply use your login credentials for immediate access.

Table of Contents

SAP HANA Starter

Welcome to *SAP HANA Starter*. This book has been especially created to provide you with all the information that you need to get set up with SAP HANA. You will learn the basics of SAP HANA, get started with building your first data model, and discover some tips and tricks for getting the most out of SAP HANA.

This document contains the following sections:

So what is SAP HANA? – find out what SAP HANA actually is, what makes it different from existing database systems, what you can do with it, and why it's so great.

Installation – learn how to download and install the SAP HANA Studio with minimum fuss and then set it up, so that you can connect it to your SAP HANA appliance and use it as soon as possible.

Quick start – this section will show you how to create a simple SAP HANA application, using attribute and analytical views—SAP HANA's basic application building blocks.

Top features you need to know about – here, you will learn how to perform the most important tasks in SAP HANA. By the end of this section, you will be able to create attribute, analytical, and calculation views, which will enable you to model any SAP HANA application you need to make. You'll also see other important features of the system, such as input prompts and filters.

People and places you should get to know – the SAP HANA community is very lively, and you can find a wealth of information in different places. This section provides you with many useful links to the product pages and forums, as well as a number of helpful articles, tutorials, blogs, and the Twitter feeds of SAP HANA gurus.

So, what is SAP HANA?

SAP is likely the largest computer software house in the world today. SAP is famous for its **Enterprise Resource Planning** (**ERP**) software, used by most of the largest companies throughout the world.

SAP's ERP system allows businesses to store just about all the information they need to function, from data related to customers, to purchase orders, to deliveries, to invoices, through to production schedules for factories, stock levels, and so on. SAP's main selling point is the real-time, integrated aspect of the system—if an incoming delivery is entered into the system, then the stock levels are updated in real time. Data is always fresh, always current.

In 1997, SAP released SAP **Business Information Warehouse** (**BIW**), its vision of a data warehouse solution for the SAP ERP system. This product has gone through several different versions, right up to the SAP **Business Warehouse** (**BW**) 7.3 version, the latest at the time of writing.

The SAP BW (Business Warehouse—the term used to describe the underlying technology, as opposed to Business Intelligence, used to describe the user-facing technologies) system allows users to report on the data stored in the ERP system, allowing anything from simple analysis to complex simulations on sales forecasts depending on different factors.

The BW system usually does not use the same exact database machine as the ERP system—data is moved from the ERP to the BW machine for reporting. This is done so as not to impact the data entry (vital) functions with someone wanting a report on last year's sales (which is less important). Hence, the data in BW (and in data warehouses in general) is not always up-to-date. Data loads are generally done once per day, introducing a slight delay in data freshness.

Note, then, the two different principal functions of SAP's software, as follows:

+ SAP ERP stores data in a database
+ SAP BW takes the data in the database, aggregates it, and presents totals and trends to the user

As we can see, the two systems will produce different loads on the system, in terms of the SQL used by the applications to "talk" to the database. The first will essentially be `INSERT` and `UPDATE` instructions, whereas the second will almost exclusively generate `SELECT` statements.

Traditionally, it has been very difficult to optimize SAP BW systems to provide satisfactory performance for reporting. Reports taking minutes or even hours to execute are not unheard of, despite optimization efforts including precalculation of aggregates, storing multiple copies of data at different detail levels, and so on.

What's more, SAP (the software) has always had to rely on third-party database software for the underlying data storage. SAP (the company) has had to field untold support calls from customers dissatisfied with the performance of the ERP and BW software, where the performance problems were largely a result of the shortcomings of the database software itself. It is to address this problem that SAP has released SAP HANA.

SAP HANA is SAP's vision of in-memory computing. Based upon several existing technologies, SAP HANA is a database system, designed to greatly speed up database accesses when reading data, while not slowing data insertion. In several real-world scenarios, SAP has managed to show speedup of more than 10 orders of magnitude, compared to previously recorded performance figures on legacy database systems. Many clients who have implemented SAP HANA have managed to achieve speedups of between 5 and 7 orders of magnitude—of course, the achieved increased speed depends on several factors, including the state of the original system, the time and effort spent transferring it to SAP HANA, and the workload. If the original system was not well designed, and the transfer to SAP HANA used as an opportunity to rework the data model, then the improvements would be greater.

HANA doesn't actually mean anything, but some people have coined the phrase **High performance ANalytical Appliance**, and as this name suggests, it is not just some software you can install. The SAP HANA system comprises both the software and the hardware necessary to function. By selling SAP HANA as a complete system of its own SAP HANA database on certified hardware supplied by partners such as IBM, HP, and Dell, SAP can guarantee some level of performance (and avoid support calls from clients who aren't getting the performance level they think they should be getting).

SAP HANA architecture

The two main parts of the SAP HANA server system are the hardware and the software. On the client side, SAP provides the SAP HANA Studio which allows application modeling.

For data reporting on a SAP HANA system, SAP's **BusinessObjects** software can connect natively to SAP HANA, and reporting can be done in any other program that can create and consume MDX queries (such as Microsoft Excel pivot tables), which SAP HANA supports natively.

This book will not go into any detail regarding the reporting software on top of SAP HANA, except to show simple Excel integration—the topic of reporting is too vast for the scope of this book, and it is covered more than adequately elsewhere.

The following diagram is an overview (provided by SAP) of the SAP HANA system architecture, showing clearly the different components and integration between them:

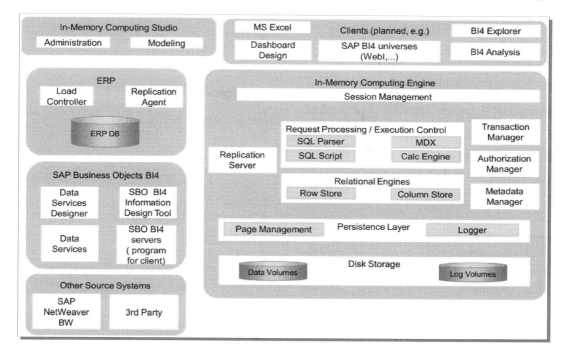

The hardware

The SAP HANA box itself is a massively multi-core, multi-CPU server, with a great deal of memory—up to several terabytes. For example, on May 16, 2012, IBM announced that in collaboration with SAP, they had built a machine with 100 TB of main memory. At the time, SAP indicated that this machine would be sufficient to run the eight largest clients of SAP ERP—all at the same time!

One of the main strong points of SAP HANA is its ability to process data in parallel, cutting the initial (large) amount of data into small chunks, and then giving each chunk to a separate CPU to work on—hence the need for the large number of CPU cores.

One other aspect of the system is that wherever possible, data is kept in memory, in order to speed up access time. Where a traditional database system might set aside a gigabyte or two of memory as a cache, SAP HANA takes this to the next level, using nearly all the server's memory for the data, making access times nearly instantaneous.

The software

The database software powering SAP HANA is what's known as a column-based RDBMS, and is a logical evolution of the following three existing technologies that were already in use at SAP:

+ **TREX**: SAP's search engine, a component of SAP NetWeaver since 2000. TREX already included in-memory and columnar store attributes, which were designed to improve performance by searching data already in main memory, and already in highly optimized data structures.

+ **MaxDB**: SAP's own RDBMS technology. MaxDB is a very capable, relatively simple (when compared to some other big players such as Oracle) RDBMS system. It is capable of running the SAP ERP or SAP BW, despite having very low system requirements and a fairly shallow learning curve. MaxDB brought in the persistence (that is, what happens when the power goes off—a crucial question for an in-memory system) and backup layers to SAP HANA.

+ **P*Time**: A lightweight, OLTP in-memory RDBMS system, acquired by SAP in 2005 when they bought Transact in Memory. P*Time provided the in-memory backbone to the SAP HANA software. It is worth noting that P*Time is a traditional row-based, not column-based, data store.

By combining these three proven technologies, SAP has managed to produce a coherent, persistent in-memory database system, known internally as **NewDB** (which says a lot about how the technology is viewed from inside SAP!).

How does a column-based database work?

In any given database, tables such as the following table exist:

Employee	Firstname	Lastname	Salary	Currency
1	Joe	Smith	35000	EUR
2	Emma	Thomson	40000	USD
3	Sam	Wiggins	42500	USD

Whereas, a traditional database system will store the data in a row-based format, as shown as follows:

```
1,Joe,Smith,35000,EUR
2,Emma,Thomson,40000,USD
3,Sam,Wiggins,42500,USD
```

A column-based RDBMS will store each column together, as shown as follows:

```
1,2,3
Joe,Emma,Sam
Smith,Thomson,Wiggins
35000,40000,42500
EUR,USD,USD
```

A column-based database will be able to more quickly scan a column of data than a row-based system. This point is especially important for data reporting (like SAP BW), and enables results to be given to the user much more quickly.

Another important aspect of a column-based RDBMS is data compression. Since all values in a column are stored together, there is the possibility of storing the value only once, alongside the number of occurrences. So in the example table we've just seen, the last column might be stored as follows:

```
EUR, 2:USD
```

This might not seem important, but in a table that contains several million lines, the space savings are potentially huge. SAP indicates that data can be compressed to between 10 percent and 25 percent of its original size. Of course, this means less data to scan through for the system—and since data is in memory, it means more data—between 4 and 10 times—can be kept in memory at once.

The full list of different strong points and weaknesses of column-based versus row-based database systems is beyond the scope of this book. Several interesting comparisons exist, and a good page to start would be the Wikipedia page concerning column-based RDBMSs, whose URL is given in the *People and places you should get to know* section.

In this section we've taken a look at the business need behind the SAP HANA product, the history of the software SAP HANA inherits from, the basic system architecture that makes up the product, as well as a fast overview of the column-based database concept.

In the next section, we'll take a look at what you need to get SAP HANA Studio up and running on your computer, so that you can start developing your first SAP HANA application.

Installation

In five easy steps, you can install the SAP HANA Studio and set it up on your system. Installation of the SAP HANA server is done by qualified technicians for certified hardware vendors—you cannot download the database software and install it on your server yourself. Hence, only client-side installation will be covered in this section.

Step 1 – What do I need?

Before you install the SAP HANA Studio on your computer, you will need to check if you have all of the required elements, listed as follows:

+ A minimum free disk space of 190 MB. The objects you create in SAP HANA will be stored on the server; they will not take any space on your machine (unless you export them).

+ A recommended memory of 1 GB. SAP HANA Studio is built upon the Eclipse IDE, which is written in Java. The more memory you have on your machine, the smoother the Studio will run.

+ Windows XP, Vista, or Windows 7, or SuSE Linux Enterprise Server 11, either the 32-bit or 64-bit version.

+ JAVA JRE 1.6 or 1.7. This needs to be installed and configured correctly or the SAP HANA Studio installer will fail. Additionally, if you have a 32-bit OS, you'll need a 32-bit Java, and a 64-bit Java for a 64-bit OS.

+ A SAP HANA server to connect to, you will need the server name or IP address, and the instance number. You should ask for this information from you client/system administrator. You will also need to make sure that the Studio can connect to the server on the port `3<instance_id>15` (for example, if the instance ID is `40`, the port `34015` needs to be reachable). Check with your network administrator for this.

Step 2 – Downloading the SAP HANA Studio

The easiest way to get hold of the SAP HANA Studio installation package is to use the SAP HANA DVD set; the Studio is available there.

If the DVD is not available, then you can use the SAP Service Marketplace **Software Download Center** link from `http://service.sap.com/swdc` to download the Studio. You will need a **SAP Service Marketplace** login to download the software. Additionally, your **SAP Service Marketplace** login needs to have a current SAP HANA installation active, or else you will see that no downloads are available. In the **Software Download Center** link, use the following path to find the download:

Software Downloads | Support packages and patches | Browse our download catalog | SAP In-Memory (SAP HANA).

A final alternative to download the Studio is to use SDN. A developer version of the studio is available at the following URL:

```
http://www.sdn.sap.com/irj/scn/index?rid=/webcontent/uuid/10e6e3ff-6081-2f10-
e690-829e62f29a26
```

You will need an SDN profile to download this file. Creating a profile is free, and requires only an e-mail address. You don't even need to be a SAP customer to create a profile on SDN.

 Download the correct version of the Studio for your OS and Java installation. If you have a 32-bit OS and Java installation, install the 32-bit version of the Studio; if not, install the 64-bit version.

Step 3 – Installing the SAP HANA Studio

Installation of the Studio is straightforward. On Windows, just run the **hdbsetup.exe** program in the installation folder, as shown in the following screenshot:

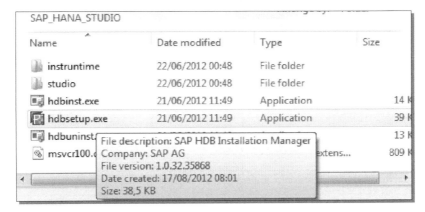

Then just follow the instructions. The only information that you'll need to provide is the destination folder for the installation, and you can usually leave the default value as it is.

Installation takes only a couple of minutes, as shown in the following image:

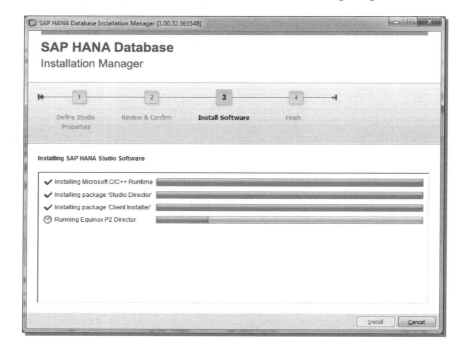

The program will be installed, and you will have a **Start** menu item created for you.

Step 4 – Your first look at the SAP HANA Studio

The first time you run the Studio after installation, you are presented with a clean, albeit rather empty interface, as shown here:

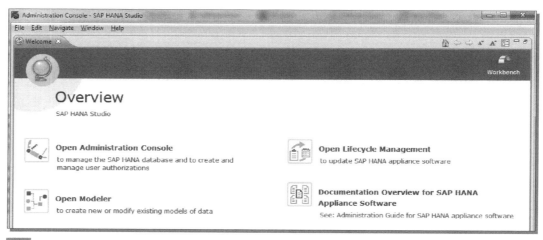

The four options available are as follows:

- **Open Administration Console**: This option allows you to administrate the SAP HANA appliance itself; for example, creating users and assigning authorizations

- **Open Modeler**: This is where you will do all your SAP HANA development work, creating views on data, running SQL queries, and so on—we'll be spending the best part of this book using the **Open Modeler** option

- **Open Lifecycle Management**: Allows you to update the SAP HANA installation on the server, by applying patches you have received from SAP

- **Documentation Overview**: This is a link to the SAP HANA online documentation pages on the sap.com website

Choose the **Open Modeler** option to get to the main development layout (referred to as a **perspective**), with which you will do most of your work in SAP HANA; the main development layout is shown in the following screenshot:

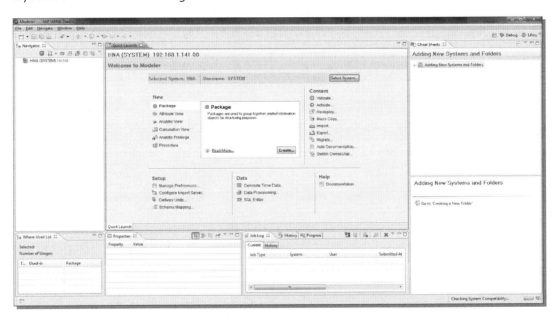

The main areas (panes) of the **Modeler** perspective are explained as follows:

- The **Navigator** pane: Shows the SAP HANA systems you've configured, as well as the list of objects (notably, tables and views) available to you on those systems.

- The **Quick Launch** pane: As its name suggests, a quick way to get to the creation screen of different object types.

✦ The **Where-Used List** pane: Readers familiar with SAP will have already come across this concept, which is widely used in the SAP ERP. This pane will show, for the object selected in the **Navigator**, where the object is used (if, for example, an attribute view is used in several analytical views, the analytical views will be listed here).

✦ The **Cheat Sheets** pane: Depending on the context (the action you're currently performing), this pane will show you different options. In the previous screenshot, we are at the main page, not performing any particular action, so this pane shows us the option to add a new SAP HANA server.

✦ The **Properties** pane: Lists, and allows modification of, the properties of the object currently being modified.

✦ The **Job Log**, **History**, and **Progress** pane: Whenever you perform creation or modification actions in SAP HANA, your changes need to be activated before being usable in the database (again, a common notion in the SAP ERP world). Since activation can take a little while (especially if you choose to use a cascaded activation, which will activate an object and then attempt activation of all dependent objects), and can potentially fail (for example, in the case of syntax errors), these panes will show you the status of your current action.

There are more panes in the SAP HANA Studio, which you can enable or disable according to your preference. The layout too is totally customizable and can be customized to suit your particular needs. Feel free to play with the Studio layout to find a layout that works for you.

If you find that you have "lost" a pane, or have made a complete mess of the layout and want to undo your changes, then go to **Window | Reset Perspective**; this will return you to the default layout at any time.

Step 5 – Configuring the Studio

Before you can do any work with the Studio, you need to connect it to your SAP HANA server. From the main **Administration Console** or **Modeler** perspective, right-click inside the **Navigator** pane, and from the menu that appears select **Add System**, which will open the following dialog window:

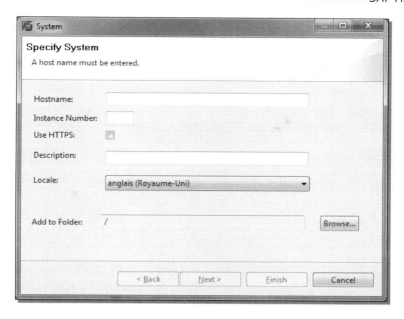

You'll need to give the hostname and instance number of your SAP HANA installation, as well as a short description (especially useful if you have several instances configured). You can also specify the **Locale** (default language) setting of your installation, and can create folders to better arrange your different SAP HANA servers.

Once that's done, click **Next >**, after which the login dialog window will open, as shown here:

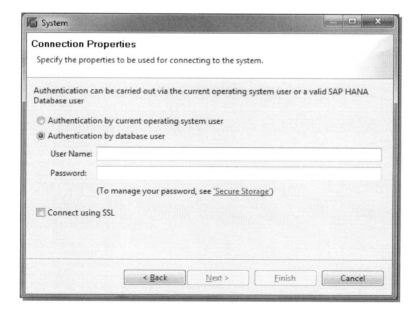

Here you are asked for your login credentials on the SAP HANA server. Ask your system administrator for this information—you might need to specify your **User Name** and **Password**, or your SAP HANA server might be configured to accept your operating system user (Single Sign-On).

You can create several entries to the same SAP HANA instance if you need to do so, for example, if you have two different sets of login credentials—an everyday user for development work, and a system administration account to create other users or perform administration tasks. If you need to do this, then the **Add to Folder** and **Description** fields can come in useful to help tell the difference.

Click on the **Finish** button to save the information.

And that's it

By this point, you should have a working installation of the SAP HANA Studio and are free to play around and discover more about it.

In the next section, we'll be taking a closer look at the **Modeler** perspective, and using it to create our first SAP HANA application.

Quick start – creating your first SAP HANA application

A SAP HANA application is where all the SAP HANA magic comes together.

Where in a "normal" reporting application (for example, SAP BW) we copy, transform, and aggregate data using transformations and intermediate storage objects (ending up with several copies of the same data), SAP HANA gives us access to transformed, aggregated views on the *original data* in the base SAP HANA tables, without going through the initial preparation steps—the necessary calculations and transformations are done on-the-fly, when the data is requested by the user.

Whenever new data becomes available in the system, it is immediately visible in reporting, since no transformation or copy is needed.

Whenever a new application is necessary, with new metrics on existing data, this application will take up practically no space on the server, since it will consist of views, and not more copies of preformatted and precalculated data.

Step 1 – The example data

In this section, we'll create a simple SAP HANA application, using the following two tables:

✦ CUSTOMERS: A list of customers, with their numerical ID and name
✦ ORDERS: A list of purchase orders, with a numerical, purchase order ID, a country code, calendar year, customer code, and order amount

The SQL statements necessary to create the tables used in this example are printed here. Readers familiar with the SQL language will see that these are simple SQL statements; just copy and paste them into the SQL editor window in the SAP HANA Studio, and the tables and data will be created for you in your local SAP HANA server. You'll then be able to follow the examples locally and recreate the views for yourself. If you don't feel like entering in the data as it's printed here, then feel free to use it as inspiration to enable you to play with the data you have in your own system.

 In a typical SAP HANA system, normally tables would not be manually created as we are doing here. Tables would usually be provided by the ERP system and loaded using a suitable ETL software (extract, transform, and load software, such as SAP's BusinessObjects Data Services, or their SLT replication server). Here, though, we'll create the tables manually, in order to more easily see the table structure and contents.

To open an SQL editor window in the HANA Studio, we click on the system name in the **Navigator** pane, then click on the **SQL** button, which is at the top of the **Navigator** pane. A text editor will open in the middle of the screen, alongside the **Quick Launch** pane.

 If you are not currently connected to a SAP HANA system, then the SQL editor window will open, but with no connection established to the database. If this should happen to you, just close and reopen the Studio and try again.

The following code creates a BOOK schema in the database, and inside that schema creates our two example tables, CUSTOMERS and ORDERS. Some simple example data is inserted into both the tables. We'll be using this sample data throughout the book to show the various features of SAP HANA:

```
create schema "BOOK";
grant select on schema "BOOK" to _SYS_REPO with grant option;
```

This instruction creates a schema, which is just a logical grouping of tables. If your SAP HANA system already contains a schema called BOOK, then this statement will fail. If this happens, just rename the schema to something else, maybe HANABOOK.

The second instruction, grant, is necessary to create views. Since we created the BOOK schema manually, the SAP HANA metadata doesn't know about it, so we have to do this bit of housekeeping ourselves. In this way, the background process of the SAP HANA studio will be able to correctly read the tables in our schema. If we don't execute this grant instruction, we won't be able to create views later, because the Studio won't have access to our tables.

```
CREATE COLUMN TABLE "BOOK"."CUSTOMERS"
  (
    "CUST_ID" INTEGER CS_INT NOT NULL ,
    "CUST_NAME" VARCHAR(25) NOT NULL ,
    "CUST_COUNTRY" VARCHAR(20)
  );
```

The previous SQL statement creates a simple table. Note that we're creating a COLUMN table (using the column-based storage). Of course, we could create a row-based table using CREATE TABLE CUSTOMERS, but that would defeat the purpose of using SAP HANA really. If you changed the name of the schema from BOOK to something else, then you'll need to change it here too.

Now, we'll put some sample data into our CUSTOMERS table, using the following SQL statements:

```
insert into "BOOK"."CUSTOMERS" values(1,'Smith','GB');
insert into "BOOK"."CUSTOMERS" values(2,'Jones','GB');
insert into "BOOK"."CUSTOMERS" values(3,'Martin','FR');
insert into "BOOK"."CUSTOMERS" values(4,'Machin','FR');
```

```
insert into "BOOK"."CUSTOMERS" values(5,'Schmidt','DE');
insert into "BOOK"."CUSTOMERS" values(6,'Muller','DE');
insert into "BOOK"."CUSTOMERS" values(7,'Garcia','ES');
insert into "BOOK"."CUSTOMERS" values(8,'Martinez','ES');
insert into "BOOK"."CUSTOMERS" values(9,'Rossi','IT');
insert into "BOOK"."CUSTOMERS" values(10,'Moretti','IT');
```

Next, we'll create our ORDERS table, again column-based, and insert its sample data using the following SQL statements:

```
CREATE COLUMN TABLE "BOOK"."ORDERS"
   (
    "ORDER_ID" INTEGER CS_INT NOT NULL ,
    "ORDER_COUNTRY" VARCHAR(20),
    "ORDER_YEAR" VARCHAR(4) NOT NULL ,
    "CUST_ID" INTEGER CS_INT NOT NULL ,
    "ORDER_AMT" INTEGER CS_INT NOT NULL
   );
insert into "BOOK"."ORDERS" values(1,'GB','2010',1,100);
insert into "BOOK"."ORDERS" values(2,'GB','2010',2,117);
insert into "BOOK"."ORDERS" values(3,'GB','2011',1,120);
insert into "BOOK"."ORDERS" values(4,'GB','2011',2,135);
insert into "BOOK"."ORDERS" values(11,'FR','2010',3,100);
insert into "BOOK"."ORDERS" values(12,'FR','2010',4,117);
insert into "BOOK"."ORDERS" values(13,'FR','2011',3,120);
insert into "BOOK"."ORDERS" values(14,'FR','2011',4,135);
insert into "BOOK"."ORDERS" values(21,'DE','2010',5,100);
insert into "BOOK"."ORDERS" values(22,'DE','2010',6,117);
insert into "BOOK"."ORDERS" values(23,'DE','2011',5,120);
insert into "BOOK"."ORDERS" values(24,'DE','2011',6,135);
insert into "BOOK"."ORDERS" values(31,'ES','2010',7,100);
insert into "BOOK"."ORDERS" values(32,'ES','2010',8,117);
insert into "BOOK"."ORDERS" values(33,'ES','2011',7,120);
insert into "BOOK"."ORDERS" values(34,'ES','2011',8,135);
insert into "BOOK"."ORDERS" values(41,'IT','2010',9,100);
insert into "BOOK"."ORDERS" values(42,'IT','2010',10,117);
insert into "BOOK"."ORDERS" values(43,'IT','2011',9,120);
insert into "BOOK"."ORDERS" values(44,'IT','2011',10,135);
```

When you have entered the SQL statements, click on the **Execute** button at the top of the SQL editor. The **Execute** button is the round green button with the right-facing arrow, which you can see in the following screenshot. The results of the instructions will be shown in the **Job Log** pane (and if you've just created a table, it'll appear in the **Navigator** pane on the left):

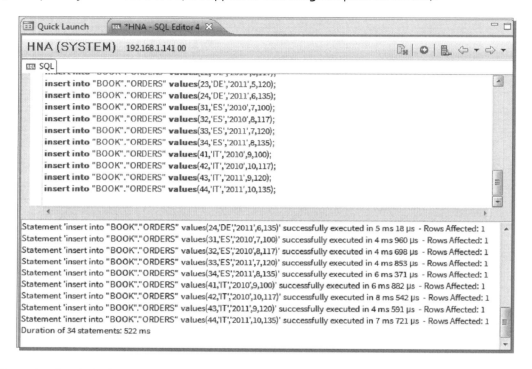

Once the data is in the SAP HANA system, we have a schema called BOOK with two tables, CUSTOMERS and ORDERS. If we refresh the **Navigator** pane by clicking on the **Catalog** node and pressing the *F5* key, our new schema will be displayed there.

Step 2 – Creating a package

Open the SAP HANA Studio now, and choose the **Modeler** perspective (go to **Window | Choose Perspective | Modeler**). You'll be presented with the main SAP HANA **Modeler** screen, which we saw in the previous section and which we'll be using from now on.

SAP HANA is a rapidly evolving piece of software—both server side and client side. It is possible that, depending on the version of the SAP HANA Studio you use, the interface might not look exactly like the screenshots in this book. Don't be alarmed at this—the concepts are the same, using the same basic objects, no matter which version of the Studio you use.

In the middle of the screen, in the **Quick Launch** panel, we have the possibility to create the most used objects in SAP HANA. In this chapter, we'll be creating the first three (package, attribute view, and analytical view). The means of creation and the usage of each of these objects will be explained in their corresponding section. In the next section, we'll look at more advanced usage of these, as well as seeing other key concepts in SAP HANA.

The first object to create is a **package**. A package is a logical grouping of objects you want to keep together. It's the same terminology you will find in SAP ERP or BW development.

Objects in different packages can be used together in the same development, so placing objects in different packages will not have any effect on the way you use them, but keeping objects that have a logical link between them will later make them easier to find. For example, you might like to keep all your development objects for the Sales Reporting project together in one package, and all your HR Reporting objects in another.

For the purpose of this book, we'll create a simple package called (rather unimaginatively) book, and we'll put our development objects in it.

From the main **Modeler** screen, in the **Quick Launch** panel, select **Package**, then press the **Create** button. A new window will open, as shown in the following screenshot:

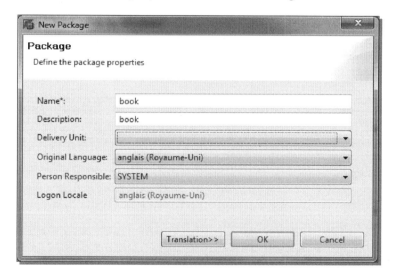

You'll be asked for a name and a description for the package—the package for this book is called **book**, with a description of **book**.

There is a field called **Delivery Unit**. A delivery unit is analogous to SAP's transport order concept, and allows you to package development objects for transporting them to other systems (such as, testing and then production). **Delivery Units** are not covered in this book, and we don't have one for this development, so leave this field blank.

Once the package has been created, the modeling objects needed for the development can be created, and stored inside it.

Step 3 – Creating an attribute view

In SAP HANA, an attribute view is used, as its name suggests, to present a view of master data to the user.

We can picture a master customer data record, where every imaginable piece of information concerning the customer is available, from their name, their date of birth, right down to the nearest post office, or the name of the railway station closest to the customer (yes, these fields really are available in SAP ERP!). Most of this information is unnecessary to the development being made and should be excluded from the view so as not to pollute the report, and so as to limit the amount of data read from the database in order to speed up the application.

Of course, we could only copy the data we're interested in to a new table and use that, but it's time-consuming, error-prone, and a maintenance nightmare to duplicate the data, when we can just have the database present only the fields we're interested in and ignore the rest.

An attribute view performs this role in SAP HANA—it can join one or more tables of master data (attributes), and present only certain fields to the user (view). Note that an attribute view can *only* use non-numeric information—you can't add numeric data to an attribute view.

In this example, we'll create a simple attribute view, selecting only certain fields for use.

The attribute view created here uses the CUSTOMERS table from the previous section. In this table, the fields CUST_ID, CUST_NAME, and CUST_COUNTRY are available, and in the attribute view created, only CUST_ID and CUST_NAME will be visible.

From the main **Modeler** perspective of the Studio, in the **Quick Launch** panel, select **Attribute View**, then click on **Create**. You can also right-click on the package in the **Content** node of the **Navigator pane**, and select **New | Attribute View**—whichever method you prefer, they both lead to the same screen, shown in the following screenshot:

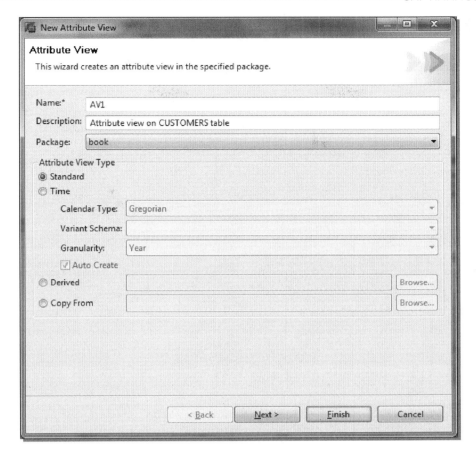

Give a name and a description for your attribute view. The **Name** field should consist of only uppercase letters, numbers, and the underscore character. The **Description** field can be anything you prefer—it's for your reference, not for SAP HANA's.

There are four different types of attribute view, explained as follows:

✦ **Standard**: This view is based on database tables.

✦ **Derived**: This view is derived from another attribute view (somewhat like the "create by reference" option for InfoObjects in SAP BW, for those who are familiar with the software)—if you create View B, derived from View A, then View B will be identical to View A. If, at a later time, you change View A, then View B will change as well.

✦ **Copy From**: Like **Derived**, this will incorporate the particularities of the original View, but is not linked to that View—if you create View B as a copy of View A, then View B will be identical to View A. If, at a later time, you change View A, then view B will not be impacted.

✦ **Time**: Finally, an attribute view can hold time information. Typically, this includes date, week, month, and year details such as which month of the year contains which week number.

Here we'll create a **Standard** View in our **book** package so just click on **Next**; where we can add table(s) to our View, a dialog window will appear, as shown in the following screenshot:

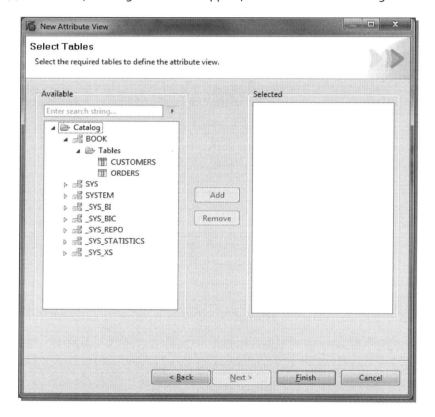

This is the SAP HANA **Select Tables** dialog window. We'll see it often when we create Views.

We can either select the table to add by exploring the tree structure until we find the table, after which we select the table and then click the **Add** button (as can be seen in the screenshot), or we can do a search by table name, as shown here:

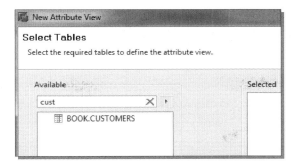

Just type the first few characters of the table name, and click on the arrow—all matching tables will be listed, and here again, select the table and then click on the **Add** button.

 We can see here that the SAP HANA Studio shows in which schema a table can be found—if we have many tables containing the letters **cust**, they would all be listed, and by seeing the schema we can select the correct table.

Several tables can be added to a view at once, just add all the tables required.

Here, we'll just add our **CUSTOMERS** table to the view—once that's done, click on **Finish** to see the results.

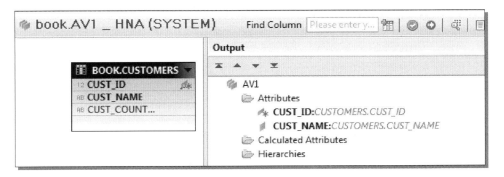

The next step in our attribute view creation is to add the fields we want to use. The **CUSTOMERS** table contains three fields; we'll only be using two of them in the view.

An attribute view contains, like a table itself, key fields and data fields. Right-click on the **CUST_ID** field in the left-hand pane, and select **Add as key attribute**. Then, add the **CUST_NAME** field as a regular attribute, using the **Add as attribute** option.

Once that's done, we have an attribute view that looks similar to the screenshot we've just seen. There's a little green star next to **CUST_ID**, to show it's a key attribute.

Before any object in SAP HANA can be used, it needs to be activated. Readers familiar with the SAP ERP development cycle will have come across this notion often.

Activation is simple—as you can see in the screenshot, at the top-right of the development pane is a round green button with a right-facing arrow. This button saves and then activates the current development object. Click this button now so that we can use our attribute view.

The results of the activation request are in the **Job Log** pane at the bottom of the screen (by default, unless you have moved or hidden it):

In order to check that our attribute view is working correctly, SAP HANA provides a **Data Preview** function. This is roughly the equivalent of the SE16 transaction in a SAP ERP system, and shows a tabular listing of the view's contents. It's a very useful debugging tool.

In the **Content** node of the **Navigator** pane, right-click the attribute view (you might need to expand the tree to see your newly created view), and select **Data Preview**. SAP HANA will present you with the contents of the view, as shown:

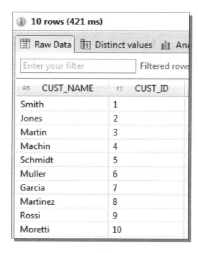

As expected, the contents of the attribute view correspond to the contents of the underlying CUSTOMERS table; however, only the two fields **CUST_ID** and **CUST_NAME** are visible in the view.

Congratulations! We've created an attribute view, one of the most important building blocks of a SAP HANA application.

Next, we'll create an analytic view, which allows us to work with numeric information from the database.

Step 4 – Creating an analytical view

In the previous section, we created an attribute view—a projection of non-numeric data, allowing us in a simple way to extract only the necessary information from the database.

As we saw, attribute views can only work with characteristic attributes—that is, meta-information, or information describing other information, such as a name, an address, and so on. Attribute views cannot work with any numerical data, such as an order amount, or a salary.

To extract figures from the database, an analytic view must be used. This view will provide a projection of numeric data, combining it (if necessary) with one or more attribute views. In this way, the analytic view will extract the figures from the underlying table, and combine them with the meta-information in the attribute view, to describe the numeric data. For readers familiar with SAP's BW platform, this is analogous to a BW Cube (analytic view) and its dimensions (attribute views).

Here, we'll create an analytic view that will use the attribute view to provide the customer's name, which can then be presented alongside the order amount value. This is much more useful to users than simply showing the order amount alongside the customer's ID.

Creation of an analytic view is done in the same way as an attribute view. From the **Quick Launch** pane of the **Modeler** perspective, click on **Analytic View** and then click on **Create** to be presented with the **New Analytic View** creation dialog:

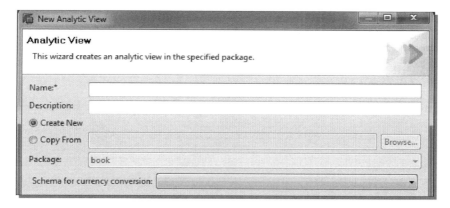

An analytic view needs to have a name and its description filled in the **Name** and **Description** field respectively. Additionally, we need to indicate to SAP HANA in which **Package** we want to store our view (our package is called **book**).

In much the same way as an attribute view, we can create our analytic view either from scratch, or by copying an existing analytic view.

In this example, we'll create a view from scratch, so just click **Next** to select the tables we wish to include in our view. You'll be presented with the **Select table** dialog window we saw in the previous section. For our analytic view, we want to add the ORDERS table from the BOOK schema. Once that's done, click **Next**, to add attribute views.

By including an attribute view in an analytic view, we can describe the numeric data. Of course, if all the information necessary was already present in our ORDERS table, we could just use the fields from the table. In our example, in order to be able to show the customer name alongside their order information, we'll be adding the attribute view that we created in the previous section. This is done using SAP HANA's **Select Attribute Views** dialog window, as shown in the following screenshot:

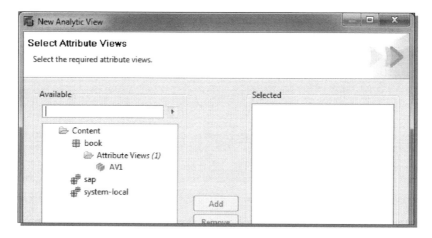

This dialog is almost identical to the **Select table** dialog window, but it allows selection of attribute views. Just add our view, then click **Next**, where we'll be able to design our analytic view with the graphical designer.

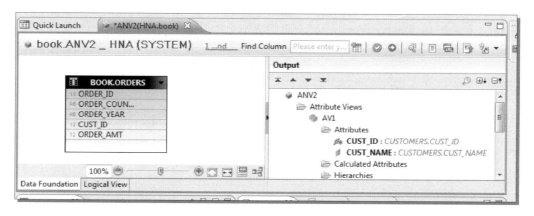

There's quite a lot of information on this screen, so let's take a look at it in detail.

First, notice that the graphical designer tab (called ***<view name>(HNA.book)**) has two tabs at the bottom of the screen—**Data Foundation** and **Logical View**. The **Data Foundation** tab is used to see what tables (note, not attribute views) and fields are available in the view. Here, for example, we can see that the ORDERS table has been added to the view—and it is the only table we selected. The **Logical View**, which we will see in a while, will show us how the fields we have selected are joined to each other.

Next, we can see that the fields from our attribute view are available for use in the analytic view, even though we can't see the attribute view on the screen. All the fields in every attribute view selected in the analytical view are automatically visible—it is enough to add the attribute view to the analytic view to have access to all its fields.

In much the same way as when we created our attribute view, an analytic view requires that we define first which table fields we wish to use. The definition is done in exactly the same way as for the attribute view, by right-clicking on the required field, and selecting **Add as attribute**.

Please add the **ORDER_YEAR**, **ORDER_ID**, and **CUST_ID** fields as attributes to our analytic view. You'll notice that in the **Output** pane, the **CUST_ID** field, which you have just added, has been renamed to **CUST_ID_1**, because an attribute named **CUST_ID** is already present in the analytic view—it was provided by the attribute view.

Adding numeric data is done in a similar way, but these fields are marked as **Measures**, not attributes; so please add the **ORDER_AMT** field as a measure. Adding a field as a measure indicates to SAP HANA (and to reporting software) that you expect to be able to do calculations on this field—for example, summing, calculating the average, finding the largest value, and so on.

You will end up with an analytic view resembling the one seen in the following screenshot:

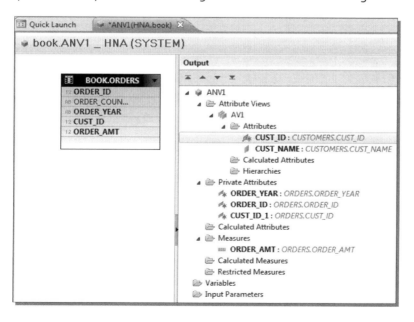

Next, we'll join our analytic view with our attribute view so that we can see the customer name (from the attribute view) alongside their order information (from the analytic view). To do this, we need to switch to the **Logical View** tab.

To join the attribute view to the **Data Foundation** tab of the analytic view, simply click on the junction field in the attribute view, and drag it to the junction field in the **Data Foundation** tab.

We'll join using the **CUST_ID** field in the attribute view, and the **CUST_ID_1** field in the **Data Foundation** tab of the analytic view, as shown in the following screenshot:

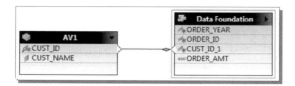

That's all that needs to be done; our analytic view has been created, and it joins the ORDERS table to the attribute view (which we created on the CUSTOMERS table). We're almost done—once the analytic view has been activated, we'll be able to see our data, so do that now. Activation of an analytic view is done in the same way as an attribute view; just click on the green save and activate button at the top right-hand corner of the analytic view development pane.

Step 5 - Previewing the data

The **Data Preview** function that we saw earlier is a more useful function when used to visualize the output of an analytic view.

Open the **Data Preview** tab for our analytic view; you will see the order information, from the ORDERS table, alongside the customer name, from the CUSTOMERS table:

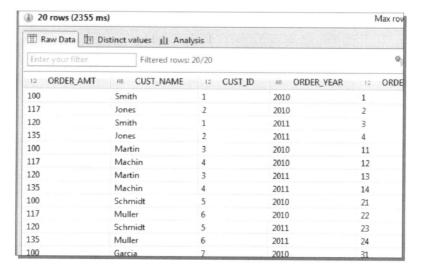

If you switch to the **Analysis** tab of **Data Preview**, however, you can see your data in a much more visual way, similar to an Excel pivot table, as shown in the following screenshot:

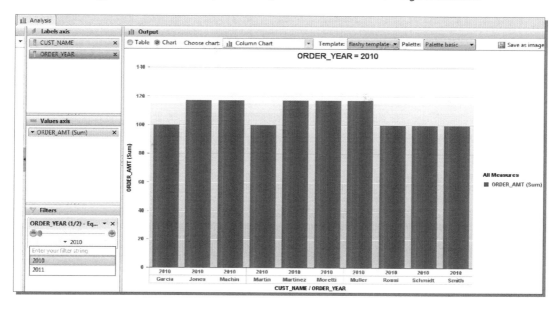

Here are some of the features we can see on the screenshot (feel free to play with the **Data Preview** tab until you are comfortable with it—you cannot break anything, and nothing that you do will be saved):

We can add fields from our view to the Labels and Values axis as we require, and here we are visualizing the **ORDER_AMT** field by the **CUST_NAME** and **ORDER_YEAR** fields.

We're using a **Column Chart** chart option—there are a number of other chart options available. We've added **ORDER_YEAR** to the **Filters** box; this has given us an automatic filter possibility, either using the slider, or the drop-down box, or by entering the value on which we wish to filter. Here, we've filtered on the year **2010**.

In this section, we've taken a look at the two basic building blocks of a SAP HANA application, the attribute view and the analytic view, using some simple data. First, we created our sample tables and data using standard SQL statements, and then we created a package to contain our two views.

We created an attribute view, which allows us to use only the fields we require from master data tables, and an analytic view, which, when combined with the attribute view, shows the numeric data we need for our reporting application.

These two types of views are the basic development objects necessary to build a SAP HANA application, and in many cases will provide the functionality you need to build your reporting application, allowing you to create complex reports while keeping only one copy of the data, and needing no special processing when new data is added to the base tables.

In the next section, we'll be taking the reporting application that we've just built together, and expanding it, using more of the development objects provided by SAP HANA to allow our users to do simulations on sales for next year, based upon the sales reported this year. To do this, we will see advanced topics, such as calculation views, user input prompts, calculated measures, as well as visualizing our reporting simulator in Microsoft Excel.

Top features you'll want to know about

As you start to use SAP HANA, you will realize that there are a wide variety of things that you can do with it. This section will teach you the most commonly performed tasks and most commonly used features in SAP HANA.

We'll be expanding on the example that we built in the last section to use the more advanced features of SAP HANA in creating a sales prevision system, using only the sample data, which we've already seen. Our prevision application (or simulator) will allow the user to enter an expected increase in sales (in percent), and then show, alongside the actual data, what that percentage increase will translate to in projected sales.

We'll be using the same tables created earlier, and just expand our reporting application—no new tables or data will be needed to create our sales simulator. The simulator will work on the original data, and present results created on-the-fly. The advantage to this is that when new data arrives in the underlying table (say we load data in from a new department), our simulator will "just work"—no rework, fiddling, or tweaking necessary.

This is a fairly common scenario in business reporting and simulation applications. We'll see that using only the standard tools available in SAP HANA, we can build this simulator relatively quickly and with little fuss.

In order to build this application, we will be using the following building blocks:

+ A second analytic view
+ A filter
+ A calculated attribute
+ An input parameter
+ A calculated measure
+ A graphical calculation view with projections and a union

Finally, we will call up our application with Microsoft Excel, displaying simple integration with SAP HANA.

Analytic view

The first thing we need to create is a second analytic view. This will enable us to compare our projected sales with the actual sales.

As we saw in the previous section, we can create an analytic view by copying an existing view, so we'll do that now.

From the **Quick Launch** pane of the **Modeler** perspective of the Studio, select **Analytic View**, then click **Create**. Select **Copy From**, then choose the analytic view, which we created in the previous section:

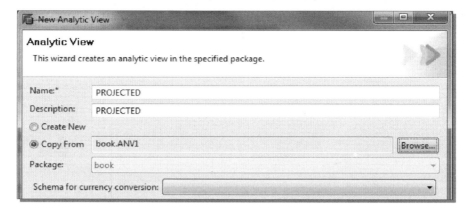

As we saw earlier, when we create an analytic view by copying another analytic view, our new view will be an identical copy of the old view. We can, however, make changes to the old view without impacting our copy.

You will be presented with a new analytic view, identical to the one we created previously.

This analytic view will be used to show the projected data, and we'll be modifying it heavily over the next few sections.

Filters

In SAP HANA, we can filter information at the lowest level—right at the database. By filtering data as close to the disk as possible, we will greatly speed up our reporting application.

In our simulator application, we're going to filter the data in our **PROJECTED** view. By default, the view will give us all data from the underlying ORDERS table, but we only want to keep data from the year **2011**.

To create a filter, in the graphical analytic view definition builder, right-click on the field name on which to filter, and select **Apply Filter**. We'll be filtering on the **ORDER_YEAR** field. SAP HANA will present us with a filter dialog, as shown in the following screenshot:

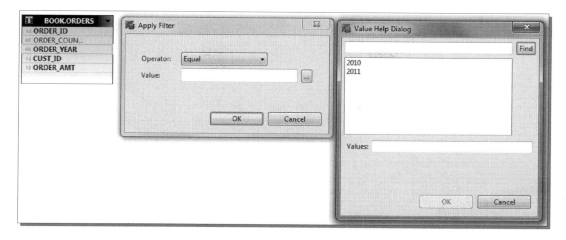

We can choose the type of filter to apply—for example, **Select all lines where the filter field has a value equal to**, or **Select all lines where the filter field has a value less than**, then we just need to give the value for comparison, and SAP HANA will do the rest.

Here, we'll select **Equal**. Next to the **Value** field is the input help button; click on that to see the **Value Help Dialog** window, which you can see in the previous screenshot. If you click on the **Find** button, SAP HANA will present a list of unique values in the view, for the field selected. Here, for our **ORDER_YEAR** field, we find our two values of **2010** and **2011**. Select the value **2011** and click **OK** to create the filter. You'll see a funnel icon in the view builder, indicating a filter is in place.

If we activate the view and then preview the data in it, we'll see that only data from **2011** is present.

Calculated attributes

Now that we have our view filtering only on data from 2011, we're going to create a new column from scratch, which will show us the year 2012. This is the base of our simulator application—we'll simulate data from 2012, based upon the data from 2011.

To do this, we're going to create a **calculated attribute**. As its name suggests, this function allows us to do calculations on attribute (non-numeric) values. For readers familiar with SAP's BW system, this feature is unique to HANA—you can't create calculated attributes (at query level) in BW, but can only create calculated measures (which are referred to as ratios or key figures).

In our example, we'll be taking the **ORDER_YEAR** value, adding one year, and storing the result in a new column that we'll call **NEXT_YEAR**.

In the **Output** pane of the analytic view, you'll see a node named **Calculated Attributes**, as we can see here:

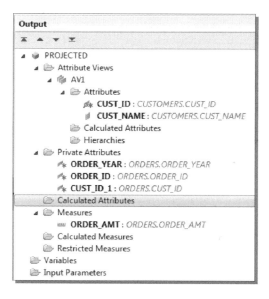

Right-click on the **Calculated Attributes** node, then select **New** from the menu. You'll see the **Calculated Attribute** dialog window, which asks for a name and a description for the attribute (we'll use **NEXT_YEAR** as both name and description). The data type for the calculated attribute is **VARCHAR** with a length of 4—this is the same type as the original **ORDER_YEAR** field.

Next, we need to enter the formula used to calculate the attribute. If you've used formulas in Excel, then this will seem familiar; it works the same way.

Basically, what we need to do is to take the value of the **ORDER_YEAR** column, and add 1. However, we can't work on the **ORDER_YEAR** column directly; as we've just seen, its data type is **VARCHAR**, which is a string of characters.

In order to do mathematical calculations on the value in the **ORDER_YEAR** column, we must first obtain a numeric representation of the value. Next, we'll add 1 to this value, and then retransform the result back into a string.

This can be summarized in the following points:

✦ Obtain a numeric representation of the contents of the **ORDER_YEAR** column
✦ Add 1
✦ Transform the result of the calculation back into a string representation

Fortunately, this is a lot easier than it sounds; SAP HANA provides a large number of functions to do different tasks—you'll see them in the **Functions** pane. Have a look at these functions; most of the function names are fairly self-explanatory, and they have been grouped together into categories (just like Excel really).The two we'll be using are `int()` and `string()`.

In the **Elements** pane, you'll see the different components (attributes, measures, calculated attributes, and so on) of the analytic view—any or all of these can be used when you create your calculation. You can even mix and match your attributes and measures. For example, you could create a **PROGRESSION** column (calculated attribute) when the sales for a year for a particular customer (**ORDER_AMT**, measure) are higher this year than their sales last year (**ORDER_YEAR**, attribute). We'll be using the private attribute, **ORDER_YEAR**.

In the **Expression Editor** window, enter `string(int("ORDER_YEAR")+1)`.

We can now add our calculated attribute, then save, activate, and do a data preview on our view to see the results.

As expected, we have a new column, called **NEXT_YEAR**, which contains the value **2012**, as shown in the following screenshot:

12 ORDER_AMT	AB CUST_NAME	12 CUST_ID	AB ORDER_YEAR	12 ORDER_ID	AB NEXT_YEAR
120	Smith	1	2011	3	2012
135	Jones	2	2011	4	2012
120	Martin	3	2011	13	2012
135	Machin	4	2011	14	2012
120	Schmidt	5	2011	23	2012
135	Muller	6	2011	24	2012
120	Garcia	7	2011	33	2012
135	Martinez	8	2011	34	2012
120	Rossi	9	2011	43	2012
135	Moretti	10	2011	44	2012

Of course, if we change the filter on the view, to filter on the year **2010** instead of **2011**, then the **NEXT_YEAR** column will take the value **2011** instead of **2012**. If you decide to check this, then please make sure you restore the filter to the default value of **2011**, or else the rest of our simulator won't work right.

Input Parameters

One of the more useful features of SAP HANA is the input parameter. This allows an application to be developed where the results depend on the input of the user at runtime. This input can be used to filter results, to perform calculations, and so on.

In our simulation application, we're going to ask the user to tell us by how much the company sales are expected to increase next year. When we run the application, we'll be asked to fill in the value, and then we can use this value to calculate our projected sales.

Creating an input parameter is a simple affair—as usual, in the **Output** pane of our analytic view, click on the **Input Parameters** node, then **New** to see the **Input Parameters** dialog, as shown in the following screenshot:

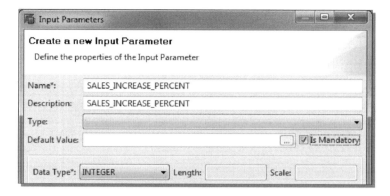

Here, we'll create a parameter called **SALES_INCREASE_PERCENT**, which is mandatory (the user will have to enter a value to be able to see the results of the view).

Because we'll be asking the user for an increase in percentage, we'll not define a type for the variable. The **Type** field indicates to SAP HANA the kind of data we'll be asking for —either an attribute value, a currency, a date, or a list of accepted values from which the user can choose. We'll be asking for none of these—we just want the user to enter a number, so leave the **Type** field empty. The **Data Type** field, however, will contain an **INTEGER** value; SAP HANA will use this information to validate that the user enters a valid value, and because it's a number, we'll be able to use it later in calculations.

 If you save the variable, activate the view, and request a data preview, you will obtain the same results as we saw earlier. Even though we defined our variable as **Is Mandatory**, we were not asked to input any value. The reason for this is quite simple—the variable exists, but it is not yet used anywhere. As soon as we integrate the variable in our view, we'll be asked to input a value.

Calculated Measures

Now that we have a variable, which the user can fill in, we can use this to create our projected sales total.

To store this amount, we need a new column in our view, and this column will be a measure, just like **ORDER_AMOUNT**. However, because this information is not present in any underlying table, it is called a calculated measure. Every time we ask SAP HANA for the contents of our view, this column will be recalculated.

Creation of a calculated measure is done in exactly the same way as a calculated attribute—right-click on **Calculated Measures** in the **Output** pane of the view, and select **New**. We are presented with exactly the same dialog as when we created our calculated attribute earlier; the only difference being that this time, instead of creating text-type columns, we are presented with a list of numeric types in the **Data Type** field.

Give the calculated measure a name and a description (**PROJECTED_SALES**) and a data type (**INTEGER**).

In the **Formula Editor** window, we want to calculate a value based on the **ORDER_AMT** field, and increase this value by the percentage amount the user enters in our **SALES_INCREASE_PERCENT** variable.

You'll see, in the same way as for the calculated attribute we created earlier, that in the **Elements** pane our **ORDER_AMT** field and **SALES_INCREASE_PERCENT** variable are available for use:

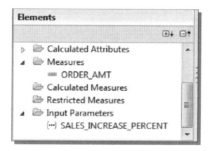

If you double-click on the field and then the variable, they'll be added to the **Formula Editor** window. **ORDER_AMT** will appear as **"ORDER_AMT"** and **SALES_INCREASE_PERCENT** will be surrounded with **$$**. These dollar signs indicate that we're talking about a variable, and that the value will be supplied at runtime.

The formula to calculate the projected sales as a percentage increase of **ORDER_AMT** is
`(("ORDER_AMT" * $$SALES_INCREASE_PERCENT$$) / 100) + "ORDER_AMT".`

Please enter this formula as it appears here into the **Formula Editor** window. Be careful with the brackets—they're important. SAP HANA will perform the calculation we enter respecting mathematical rules of precedence; the brackets make sure calculations are done in the order we specify (notably that the multiplication is done before the division)—if not, then the values will be divided by `100` before being multiplied by the percentage increase, and since the fields are of type **INTEGER**, the result will be `0`.

Once that's done, save the calculated measure, and reactivate the analytic view.

Your view should at this point look like the one displayed in the following screenshot:

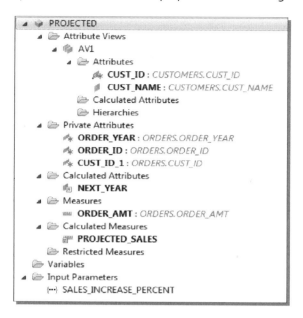

Starting to look fairly full, isn't it?

If we now request a data preview on our view, we obtain an input prompt, asking us for a value for the **SALES_INCREASE_PERCENT** variable, as shown here:

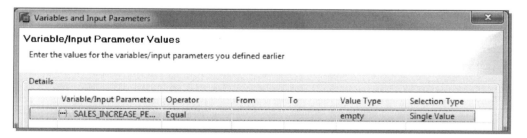

If we enter the value 10 in the **From** field, and click **OK**, we can see the results of our calculations, as shown in the following screenshot:

Raw Data	Distinct values	Analysis					
Enter your filter		Filtered rows: 10/10					

ORDER_AMT	PROJECTED_SALES	CUST_NAME	CUST_ID	ORDER_YEAR	ORDER_ID	NEXT_YEAR
120	132	Smith	1	2011	3	2012
135	148	Jones	2	2011	4	2012
120	132	Martin	3	2011	13	2012
135	148	Machin	4	2011	14	2012
120	132	Schmidt	5	2011	23	2012
135	148	Muller	6	2011	24	2012
120	132	Garcia	7	2011	33	2012
135	148	Martinez	8	2011	34	2012
120	132	Rossi	9	2011	43	2012
135	148	Moretti	10	2011	44	2012

As we can see in the previous screenshot, we have a new column, called **PROJECTED_SALES**, and it contains the value of the **ORDER_AMT** column, increased by the value of the **SALES_INCREASE_PERCENT** variable—in this case 10 percent. If you refresh the data preview, you will once again be asked for the input variable—try playing with different values to check if the calculation really is done each time the data is refreshed, and that it calculates the results correctly.

Note the results for the sales value of the customer **Moretti**. In **2011** their sales were **135**. We asked for an increase of 10 percent, which is 13.5. The result of the projected sales column, however, is only **148**. SAP HANA rounds the value *down*, not *up* as we might expect. The reason is simple—like we explained earlier, the field is of the type **INTEGER**—so the best we can get when we calculate 10 percent of 135 is 13. If you require mathematically correct results, use a different data type for your columns, such as **DECIMAL**, **NUMERIC**, **REAL**, or **FLOAT**, and specify the number of decimal places you require.

Let's take a quick look at what we've built so far. In the previous section, we created two tables containing customer and order information, an attribute view allowing us to recover the customer name, and an analytic view that joins the customer name to their order information. In this section, we've added a second analytic view that will show projected sales for the year **2012**, based upon the actual sales of **2011**, increased by a user-entered percentage. To do this we created a filter, calculated attribute, input parameter, and a calculated measure.

We are now in a position to join all this information together and create our sales simulator, showing the real data from **2010** and **2011**, and projected sales for **2012**.

Graphical Calculation View

In order to tie all our views together, we're going to use a graphical calculation view. This tool lets us pick and choose fields from one or more analytic views, perform joins and unions on these views, and present the results to the user.

The easiest way to understand how a graphical calculation view works is by building one. From the **Quick Launch** pane, select **Calculation View**, then **Create**.

Calculation views can be either **Graphical**, or can use **SQL Script**, an SQL-based programming language proposed by SAP for the HANA database. **SQL Script** calculation views are more powerful, since they provide more features than graphical views, but they are also more complex. **SQL Script**-based views are not covered in this book.

The **Calculation View** dialog will appear as follows:

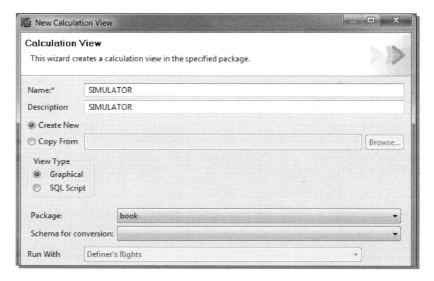

Our view will be called **SIMULATOR**, is of type **Graphical**, and is in the **book** package.

Click on **Next**, to see the now-familiar view-selection dialog. In our calculation view, we'll be combining the output of the first analytic view we created, plus our **PROJECTED** view, so please add both of those to the calculation view.

In order to define our calculation view, we are presented with a graphical designer, which initially will show only the two input nodes (our analytic views) and an **Output** node, as shown in the following screenshot:

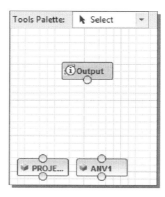

Note that by default, the input has no link to the output—we have to define the junctions ourselves.

In **Tools Palette** at the top of the graphical designer, we can see the types of building blocks available for calculation views; in our example, we'll be using two **Projection** blocks and a **Union** block.

The **Projection** blocks allow us to select only certain fields from the analytic view to use in our calculation view—once more following the principle of "filter the data as soon as possible and work with as little of it as is necessary" in order to speed up calculations. The **Projection** block also allows us to add calculated columns—these are the same as calculated attributes or measures in the analytic view; however, they are visible only in *this* calculation view, not everywhere the analytic view is present.

In order to combine the results of the two analytic views, we need to either add a **Join** or a **Union** block to the calculation view. Both of these can do the job of combining the data; however, since we need no special handling of the data (for readers who are familiar with SQL, we do not need a special join type, we're just doing a regular inner join), a **Union** block is recommended by SAP as it's faster.

The first thing we need to do is add a **Projection** block to the view, then link the upper junction of our "real data" analytic view to the lower junction point of the **Projection** block—simply by dragging a line between them. The junction points are the small circles at the top and bottom of the blocks. Click inside the circle of the source block, and drag to the circle of the destination block, as shown in the following screenshot:

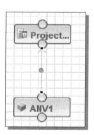

Note the direction of the arrow! Also be careful to work on the first analytic view we created, not the projected sales view—we'll get to that one in a minute.

Once this is done, click on the **Projection** block, and we are given the list of fields in the analytic view; here we can choose with which fields we would like to work.

As usual in the SAP HANA Studio, right-click on a field name, and choose **Add to Output** to select a field. To remove a field added in error, right-click on it in the **Output** pane, and select **Remove**.

In our simulator, we'll be working with the **ORDER_YEAR**, **CUST_NAME**, and **ORDER_AMT** fields, so please add these to the **Output** pane.

Next, we're going to create a calculated column, which will indicate that the data in this projection is **REAL** data.

Right-click on **Calculated Columns** in the **Output** pane, and select **New**. The **Calculated Column** dialog (identical to the **Calculated Attribute** dialog and the **Calculated Measure** dialog) will appear, as shown in the following screenshot:

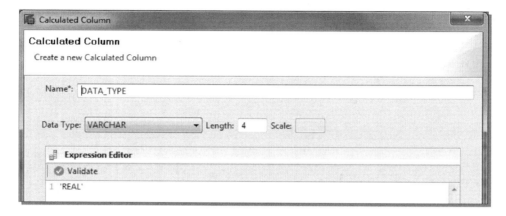

Our calculated column should be created as specified in this screenshot. It's a text-type field, which contains the value **REAL**.

> The expression used to indicate the value **REAL** just contains the word **REAL**, in single quotes, as shown in the screenshot.

Click **Add** to complete creation of the calculated column.

Now we need to add a second projection; join it to the **PROJECTED** view, and define our output columns. For the **REAL** data in the projection we just created, we used the **ORDER_YEAR** field from the underlying analytic view. For our **PROJECTED** data, we will use the **NEXT_YEAR** field, instead of **ORDER_YEAR**, since **NEXT_YEAR** contains the projected year value. Likewise, **ORDER_AMT** will be replaced with **PROJECTED_SALES**. Please add these fields to the **Output** pane.

In this projection too, we will create a calculated column, just like in the first projection, only this time it will take the value PROJ. Please do this now, using the instructions given to create the **REAL** calculated column in the first projection.

Our projections are now ready—one containing the current real data, the other containing the projected data for the value **2012**—we can now merge the data from them into one unified view, ready for consumption.

In order to do this, add a **Union** block to the view, above the two **Projection** blocks, and join them. This is done, again, by drawing a line from the upper junction of the projection nodes to the lower junction point of the output node, as shown in the following screenshot:

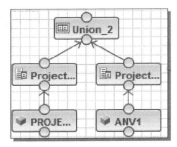

Now that we have a **Union** block, we need to make the different fields from the underlying analytic views point to the correct output fields.

Click on the **Union** block, and you will see a list of all the available fields, from both projections. Add the following fields to the target from the projection that contains the **Real** data (usually called **Projection_1**) by right-clicking on each field in turn and selecting **Add to target**:

- ✦ DATA_TYPE
- ✦ ORDER_YEAR
- ✦ ORDER_AMT
- ✦ CUST_NAME

In order to join the data from the "projected data" view, we need to map its fields to those of the "real data" view—this is done by right-clicking on the field and selecting **Map to Target**, then by selecting the appropriate output column. We need to make the following column mappings in our view:

- ✦ **DATA_TYPE** maps to **DATA_TYPE**
- ✦ **CUST_NAME** maps to **CUST_NAME**
- ✦ **PROJECTED_SALES** maps to **ORDER_AMT**
- ✦ **NEXT_YEAR** maps to **ORDER_YEAR**

Once this has been done, you should end up with a union mapping that looks like the one displayed in the following screenshot:

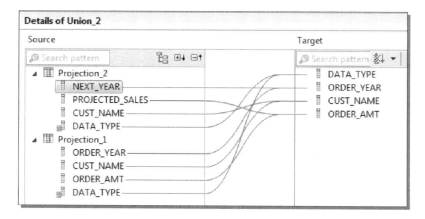

Who said spaghetti?

The final step that needs to be done is to add the union's **Target** fields to the **Output** node. Join the **Union** block and the **Output** block, then click on the **Output** block to define the fields used.

Add **DATA_TYPE**, **CUST_NAME**, and **ORDER_YEAR** as attributes, and **ORDER_AMT** as a measure.

Once this is done, check if your final calculation view looks like the one displayed in the following screenshot:

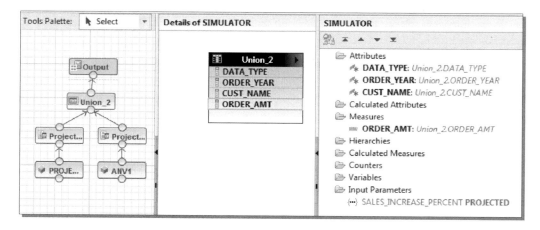

And now the moment of truth! Activate the calculation view, open a data preview, and you should be able, using the **Analysis** function, to obtain the following output:

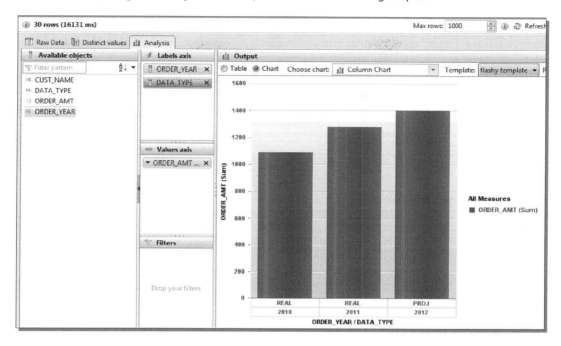

And our simulator is done! With only two tables, and using the standard building blocks available in SAP HANA, we have built a sales simulator, allowing our user to enter a projected sales increase percentage, and showing the projected data (which is created on-the-fly by SAP HANA) alongside the real data stored in the database.

SAP HANA integration with Microsoft Excel

Now that our application is finished inside SAP HANA, and we can see that it performs as expected inside the Studio, we need to be able to deploy it to our users. Asking them to use the Studio is not really practical, and we don't necessarily want to put the modeling software in the hands of all our users.

Reporting in SAP HANA can be done in most of SAP's BusinessObjects suite of applications, or in tools that can create and consume MDX queries and data.

The simplest of these tools to start with is probably Microsoft Excel. Excel can connect to SAP HANA using the MDX language (a kind of multidimensional SQL) in the form of pivot tables. These in turn allow users to "slice and dice" data as they require, to extract the metrics that they need.

There are (at the time of writing) limitations to the integration with SAP HANA and external reporting tools. These limitations are due to the relative youth of the HANA product, and are being addressed with each successive update to the software. Those listed here are valid for SAP HANA SP04; they may or may not be valid for your version.

Hierarchies (not covered in this book) can only be visualized in Microsoft Excel, not in BusinessObjects.

Prompts can only be used in BusinessObjects BI4. Views that use variables can be used in other tools, but only if the variable has a default value (if you don't have a default value on the variable, then Excel, notably, will complain that the view has been changed on the server—if your **SALES_INCREASE_PERCENT** prompt doesn't have a default value and if we didn't initially give it one—you might like to edit it now, and enter one if you wish to visualize your simulator in Excel).

In order to make MDX connections to SAP HANA, the SAP HANA client software is needed. This is separate from the Studio, and must be installed on the client workstation.

Like the Studio itself, it can be found on the SAP HANA DVD set, or in the SWDC (see the *Installation* section for full details). Additionally, like the Studio, SAP provides a developer download of the client software on SDN, at the following link:

```
http://www.sdn.sap.com/irj/scn/go/portal/prtroot/docs/webcontent/
uuid/402aa158-6a7a-2f10-0195-f43595f6fe5f.
```

Just download the appropriate version for your Microsoft Office installation.

 Even if your computer has a 64-bit installation of Windows, you most likely have a 32-bit installation of Office, and you'll need the 32-bit version of the SAP HANA client software. If you're not sure, you can find the information by going to **Help | About** dialog box. In Excel 2010, for example, click on the **File** tab, then the **Help** menu entry.

The version is specified on the right-hand side of the page, as shown in the following screenshot:

Just install the client software like you installed the Studio, usually to the default location.

Once the software is installed, there is no shortcut created on your desktop, and no entry will be created in your **Start** menu, so don't be surprised not to see anything to run.

We're going to incorporate our sales simulator in Microsoft Excel, so launch Excel.

Go to the **Data** tab, and click on **From Other Sources**, then **From Data Connection Wizard**, as shown in the following screenshot:

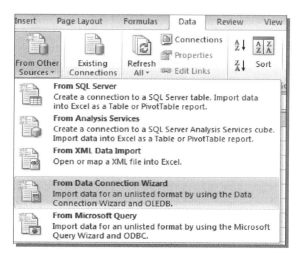

Next, select **Other/Advanced**, then select **SAP HANA MDX Provider**, and then click **Next**.

The SAP HANA Login dialog will appear, so enter your host, instance, and login information (the information you needed to connect to SAP HANA with the Studio, back in the *Installation* section).

Click on **Test Connection** to validate the connection. If the test succeeds, click on **OK** to choose the cube to which you want to connect. In Excel, all our analytic and calculation views are considered to the cubes. Choose **SIMULATOR** and click **Next**, shown in the following screenshot:

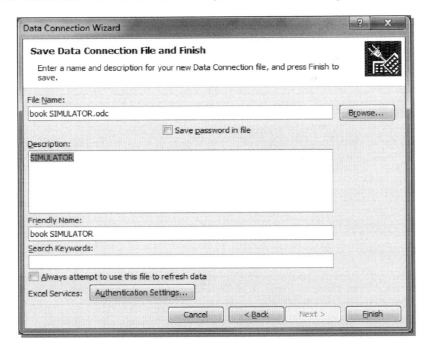

On this screen there's a **Save password in file** checkbox—this will avoid having to enter the SAP HANA password every time the Excel file is opened, but the password is stored in the Excel file, which is a little less secure.

Click on the **Finish** button to create the connection to SAP HANA, and our **SIMULATOR** view.

On the next screen, you'll be asked where you want to insert the pivot table; just click on **OK**, to see the following results:

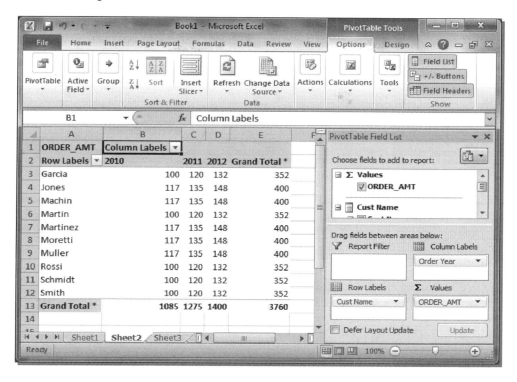

Congratulations! We now have our reporting application available in Microsoft Excel, showing the same information that we could see using the **Data Preview** feature of the SAP HANA Studio.

Note, as explained earlier, we weren't asked for the percentage increase variable because variables are not supported in Microsoft Excel—SAP HANA has used the default value of 10 percent for the variable.

In this section, we built upon the attribute and analytic views created previously. We created a second analytic view by copying the first, and added a filter, an input variable (prompt), calculated attribute, and a measure, to enable our users to project sales for 2012 based upon real sales in **2011**. Next, we created a graphical calculation view, where we used two **Projection** blocks, each containing a calculated column indicating whether the data presented was real or projected data. We added a **Union** block to the calculation view to join the data from the two projections together. In the **Union** block, we used the **ORDER_YEAR** field from the **REAL** data, mapped with the **NEXT_YEAR** field from the **PROJECTED** data, showing that we can aggregate data from different views if the field names are not the same.

Finally, we called up our simulator application in Microsoft Excel using a pivot table to report on our data, showing the integration between SAP HANA and reporting tools, using MDX.

Over the course of the last 60 pages or so, we've taken a quick look at the basic building blocks SAP HANA provides in order to allow creation of analysis applications upon the SAP HANA database. We have seen that, although based upon two very simple tables, complex reporting applications can be built using the standard building blocks.

Using the techniques found in this book, you are now in a position to build your own reporting applications, using your own data and the possibilities SAP HANA provides.

Good luck!

People and places you should get to know

If you need help with SAP HANA, here are some people and places that will prove invaluable.

Official sites

The following are a list of important sites, which will prove useful:

- **Homepage:** `http://www.sap.com/solutions/technology/in-memory-computing-platform/hana/overview/index.epx`. There's a lot of marketing material, but this is where it all starts in the SAP HANA world.

- **SAP's user review of SAP HANA:** `http://www.sap.com/solutions/technology/in-memory-computing-platform/reviews/index.epx`. Again, beware the marketing skew to the articles (this is a `sap.com` page after all), but gives good insight into the different business areas in which clients are using SAP HANA.

- **Manual and documentation:** `http://help.sap.com/hana_appliance/`. Gives release notes to the latest versions of the system, including new features and bug fixes. Additionally, most of the system manuals are available for download here.

- **SapHana minisite:** `https://www.saphana.com/community/blogs`. This site is SAP's community-facing minisite dedicated to the SAP HANA product, with blogs, user testimonials, forums, documentation, use-cases, and so on. It contains a wealth of information.

- **Knowledge base:** `http://service.sap.com/notes`. SAP notes on all aspects of the ERP, BW, and HANA products can be found here. Search for HANA. If you think you've found a bug, or the system is behaving strangely, then there's likely a note on your problem on this site. Phrasing your question right to find the note can sometimes be tricky. You'll need a SAP Service Marketplace login (S-user) to use this site.

Articles and tutorials

The following are a list of important tutorial sites, which will prove useful:

- **The Wikipedia article explaining column-based databases:** `http://en.wikipedia.org/wiki/Column-oriented_DBMS`. This article is a great place to start to get a better understanding of the underlying data storage technology used in SAP HANA, and why it brings increased performance for reporting.

- **SCN developer center:** `http://scn.sap.com/community/developer-center/hana`. Contains downloads, tutorials, and articles aimed at developers on SAP's HANA platform, including direct download links to PDF versions of the different developer manuals.

Community

The following are a list of important community sites, which will prove useful:

- **SCN Community page**: `http://scn.sap.com/community/hana-in-memory`. Start here for a wealth of information from the SAP HANA client and consultant community. If you have a question, the answer will most probably be in this site, somewhere.
- **SAP HANA's Facebook pages**: `https://www.facebook.com/HANAbySAP` and `https://www.facebook.com/Saptechnology`. A great deal of links to useful and interesting content coming from the SAP HANA team.
- **User FAQ**: `https://www.experiencesaphana.com/docs/DOC-1061`. As the name suggests, this site contains frequently asked questions regarding SAP HANA.

Blogs

The following are a list of important blogs, which will prove useful:

- **Mark Walker's personal blog**: `http://mswalker.im`. Contains anything and everything that passes through the author's mind. Lots of SAP BW and SAP HANA tidbits.
- **Thomas Zurek's personal blog**: `http://tfxz.wordpress.com/`. The blog of Thomas Zurek, VP, SAP In-Memory Platform BW.
- **Censio's SAP HANA blog section** : `http://blog.censio.fr/sap/sap-hana/`. Censio is the company the author works for, and our blog has a dedicated SAP HANA section where we share thoughts, insight, and tips and tricks. Lots of content written by the author of this book, in French.
- **The blogs of the SAP HANA team at SAP**: `https://www.saphana.com/community/blogs`. Contains useful nuggets of information, alongside a fair amount of marketing info.

Twitter

Some useful Twitter handles are as follows:

- **SAP's official account for in-memory applications**. A horde of information, and links to useful applications, webinars, and more at `https://twitter.com/SAPInMemory`
- **Follow Thomas Zurek on Twitter**: His Twitter handle is `http://twitter.com/#!/tfzx`

For more information about Packt Publishing, follow Packt Publishing at `http://twitter.com/#!/packpub`.

Thank you for buying
SAP HANA Starter

About Packt Publishing

Packt, pronounced 'packed', published its first book "Mastering phpMyAdmin for Effective MySQL Management" in April 2004 and subsequently continued to specialize in publishing highly focused books on specific technologies and solutions.

Our books and publications share the experiences of your fellow IT professionals in adapting and customizing today's systems, applications, and frameworks. Our solution based books give you the knowledge and power to customize the software and technologies you're using to get the job done. Packt books are more specific and less general than the IT books you have seen in the past. Our unique business model allows us to bring you more focused information, giving you more of what you need to know, and less of what you don't.

Packt is a modern, yet unique publishing company, which focuses on producing quality, cutting-edge books for communities of developers, administrators, and newbies alike. For more information, please visit our website: www.packtpub.com.

About Packt Enterprise

In 2010, Packt launched two new brands, Packt Enterprise and Packt Open Source, in order to continue its focus on specialization. This book is part of the Packt Enterprise brand, home to books published on enterprise software – software created by major vendors, including (but not limited to) IBM, Microsoft and Oracle, often for use in other corporations. Its titles will offer information relevant to a range of users of this software, including administrators, developers, architects, and end users.

Writing for Packt

We welcome all inquiries from people who are interested in authoring. Book proposals should be sent to author@packtpub.com. If your book idea is still at an early stage and you would like to discuss it first before writing a formal book proposal, contact us; one of our commissioning editors will get in touch with you.

We're not just looking for published authors; if you have strong technical skills but no writing experience, our experienced editors can help you develop a writing career, or simply get some additional reward for your expertise.

SAP BusinessObjects Dashboards 4.0 Cookbook

ISBN: 978-1-84968-178-0   Paperback: 352 pages

Over 90 simple and incredibly effective recipes for transforming your business data into exciting dashboards with SAP BusinessObjects Dashboards 4.0 Xcelsius

1. Learn valuable Dashboard Design best practices and tips through easy to follow recipes

2. Become skilled in using and configuring all Dashboard Design components

3. Learn how to apply Dynamic Visibility to enhance your dashboards

4. Get introduced to the most important add-ons available for Dashboard Design with the most up to date information for Dashboards 4.0

Mastering SQL Queries for SAP Business One

ISBN: 978-1-84968-236-7   Paperback: 352 pages

Utilize the power of SQL queries to bring Business Intelligence to your small to medium-sized business

1. Practical SAP query examples from an SAP Business One expert

2. Detailed steps to create and troubleshoot SQL queries for Alerts, Approvals, Formatted Searches, and Crystal Reports

3. Understand the importance and benefit of keeping SQL queries simple and easy to understand

Please check **www.PacktPub.com** for information on our titles

SAP Business ONE Implementation

ISBN: 978-1-84719-638-5   Paperback: 320 pages

Bring the power of SAP Enterprise Resource Planning to your small-to-midsize business

1. Get SAP B1 up and running quickly, optimize your business, inventory, and manage your warehouse

2. Understand how to run reports and take advantage of real-time information

3. Complete an express implementation from start to finish

4. Real-world examples with step-by-step explanations

SAP NetWeaver MDM 7.1 Administrator's Guide

ISBN: 978-1-84968-214-5   Paperback: 336 pages

Don't just manage-excel at managing your master data with SAP NetWeaver MDM 7.1

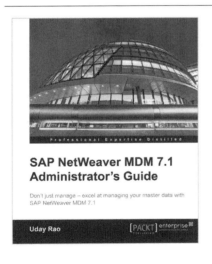

1. Written in an easy-to-follow manner, and in simple language

2. Step-by-step procedures that take you from basic to advanced administration of SAP MDM in no time

3. Learn various techniques for effectively managing master data using SAP MDM 7.1 with illustrative screen shots

Please check **www.PacktPub.com** for information on our titles

10273378R00039

Made in the USA
San Bernardino, CA
09 April 2014